OPERATING
IN THE
COURT OF
ANGELS

OPERATING
IN THE
COURT OF
ANGELS

PRAYING MEDIC

INKITY
PRESS™

Inkity Press, 137 East Elliot Road, #2292, Gilbert, AZ 85234

This book and other Inkity Press titles can be found at:
InkityPress.com and **PrayingMedic.com**

Available from Amazon.com,
CreateSpace.com, and other retail outlets.

For more information visit our website at **www.inkitypress.com** or email us at **admin@inkitypress.com** or admin@prayingmedic.com

ISBN-13: 978-0998091242 (Inkity Press)
ISBN-10: 0998091243

Printed in the U.S.A.

ACKNOWLEDGMENTS

I WOULD LIKE TO thank the many people who helped in the development of this book by providing feedback during my public discussions and by leaving comments on the articles I've posted. You know who you are. I greatly value your experiences, your insights and your encouragement.

I'd like to thank my talented wife, Denise, for her editorial help with the manuscript and for her design of the book interior and cover.

TABLE OF CONTENTS

INTRODUCTION

THE FIRST BOOK IN this series, *Defeating Your Adversary in the Court of Heaven*, has enjoyed great popularity since its publication. Not long after it went to print, I began receiving testimonies from readers who, after having visited the Court of Accusation, paid a visit to the Court of Angels. It wasn't long before readers began asking if I would consider writing a book on the Court of Angels, too.

The first book in this series provides some information not found in this one but this book is intended to stand on its own. I'll repeat some of the information from the first book in this volume. For those who are unfamiliar with the Courts of Heaven, it will provide helpful background information. For those who have already read the first book, it will serve as a review.

CHAPTER ONE

WHAT ARE
ANGELS?

THIS BOOK, THOUGH IT discusses the subject of angels, is first and foremost about Jesus. Any book about angels that does not lead you into a closer relationship with the Lord is missing the bigger picture and may be more of a distraction than a tool for growth. Your understanding of angels is worth developing, but your relationship with Jesus should be the highest priority.

It was God's intention from the moment of creation that man should rule over the earth as ambassadors who functioned under His authority (see Gen. 1:26). Because of the fall, Satan was able to usurp the rightful rule away from man. But as promised in Genesis 3:15, God's Son broke the power of Satan's rule in His incarnation, death, resurrection, and ascension (see Heb. 2:9-14). Jesus restored to us that which God had always intended. We are now able to live as mature sons of God and rule and reign over the earth the way He intended.

In the first chapter of the book of Hebrews, the writer compared Jesus with the angels. The Jews were evidently, well acquainted with the nature of angels but not with the true nature of the Messiah. The writer reviewed common knowledge about angels and then contrasted that with what had been revealed about Jesus. His point was that Jesus was far superior to any angel that was ever created. Jesus, unlike the angels, was *begotten* and not created. In verse 14, referring to the angels, the writer asked the following rhetorical question:

> *And of the angels He says:*
> *"Who makes His angels spirits*
> *And His ministers a flame of fire."*
> *Are they not all ministering spirits sent forth*
> *to minister for those who will inherit salvation?*
> *(Heb 1:7, 14)*

The word *ministering* is translated from the Greek word *leitourgikos*—the performance of service to others. Angels are servants to a particular group of people—those who will inherit salvation. If you've accepted Jesus as your savior, the angels are your servants. And even if you haven't, they're still active in your life, whether you're aware of it or not.

Angels were intimately involved in the life of Jesus. They foretold His birth (Mt 1:20) and then announced his arrival (Lk 2:8-15). An angel warned Joseph to take Mary and Jesus and flee into Egypt. An angel also instructed them to return to Israel after Herod died (Mt. 2:13-20). They ministered to Jesus after His temptation in the Judean wilderness (Mt 4:11) and in the Garden of Gethsemane (Lk 22:43). An angel rolled away the stone from His tomb and announced His resurrection (Mt 28:1-7). Angels will be responsible for separating true believers from false ones at the second coming of Christ (Mt. 13:39-40).

Angels can bring answers to prayer (Acts 12:5-10), help bring people to the knowledge of the Lord (Acts 8:26; 10:3), encourage us in times of danger (Acts 27:23-24) and care for us at our time of death (Lk 16:22).

Many of the things we experience, such as healing and deliverance, are not done directly by God but through the ministry of angels. God is not required to use angels; He could do anything He wanted directly. But He's chosen to use them to accomplish many of His works. Since He has chosen to use them as ministers of His plan, doesn't it make sense for us to learn how to cooperate with them?

The writer of the book of Hebrews wrote:

> *"Do not neglect to show hospitality to strangers, for by this some have entertained angels without knowing it." (Heb 13:2 NIV)*

The point the writer made wasn't that we ought to be gracious to humans, (although this is true) but that we ought to be considerate and welcoming to *angels* because they are God's ministers and we co-labor with them. There are more than 200 references to angels in the Bible. They were present during the creation of the earth and played key roles in some of the most important events in history. But they also interact with average people like you and I every day. Here are some characteristics of angels as recorded in the scriptures.

Angels are:

- Created beings (Ez 28:14-15)
- Obedient (Ps 103:20, Mt 6:10)
- Patient (Num 11:22-35)
- Meek (2 Pet 2:11)
- Joyful (Lk 15:1-10)
- Modest (1 Cor 11:10)
- Holy (Mk 8:38)
- Glorious (Lk 9:26)
- Immortal (Lk 20:36)

- Mighty and powerful (1 Thes 1:7-10, Rev 18:1)
- Intelligent and wise (2 Sam 14:20, 19:27, Mt 24:3)

The Bible says that angels:

- Need no rest (Rev 4:8)
- Have free will (Isa 14:12-14)
- Can appear selectively (Num 22:31)
- Can speak different languages (Rev 14:6)
- Have spiritual bodies (Heb 13:2, Jud 13:6)
- Can appear as men (Gen. 19: 1, 5, 8, 10)
- Can ascend and descend from heaven to earth (Gen 28:12, Jn 1:51)
- Can eat food (Num 22:35; 19:3; Ps 78:25)
- Have limited knowledge (Gen 18:21)
- Can travel at incredible speed (Mt 18:10)
- Can be delayed (Dan 10:12-13)

Guardian Angels

The idea that we have personal (or guardian) angels is implied in Psalm 91:

Because you have made the Lord,
who is my refuge,
Even the Most High, your dwelling place,
No evil shall befall you,

Nor shall any plague come near your dwelling;
For He shall give His angels charge over you,
To keep you in all your ways.
In their hands they shall bear you up,
Lest you dash your foot against a stone.
You shall tread upon the lion and the cobra,
The young lion and the serpent you
shall trample underfoot. (Ps 91:9-13)

Jesus suggested that we have personal angels:

And He called a child to Himself and stood him in
their midst... "See that you do not despise one of
these little ones, for I say to you, that their angels
in heaven continually behold the face of My Father
who is in Heaven." (Matt. 18:2,10)

There are many different types of angels. Each kind is created with certain abilities that other kinds do not have.

Classification and Ranking of Angels

Angels are organized into various ranks and orders. One purpose is for battle, but they are also given governmental classifications. Jude's observation about the angels who left their "domain" (NASB) or "positions of authority" (NIV) in Jude 6 is one example. Michael is called the "Archangel" or "chief angel" in Jude 9 and in Daniel 10:13, he is called one of the "chief princes."

Below are some of the terms used in the New Testament to describe the ranks of angels:

- Principalities, *Archē*, the highest rank of angels (Rom. 8:38; Eph. 1:21; 3:10; 6:12; Col. 1:16; 2:10, 15)

- Powers, *Kosmokratōr* (Eph 6:12)

- Authorities, *Exousia* (Eph. 1:21; 2:2; 3:10; 6:12; Col. 1:16; 2:10, 15; 1 Peter 3:22)

- Dominions, Kyriotēs (Eph. 1:21; Col. 1:16; 2 Peter 2:10)

- Thrones, *Thronos* (Col 1:16)

Next, we'll look at a few angels mentioned in the Bible and their unique ministries.

Michael

One of the most frequently mentioned angels in the Bible is Michael. His name means "who is like God?" He typifies warring angels and one of his chief assignments is defending the nation of Israel:

> *At that time Michael shall stand up, the great prince who stands watch over the sons of your people. (Dan 12:1)*

Michael has command over a multitude of warring angels:

> *And war broke out in heaven: Michael and **his** angels fought with the dragon; and the dragon and his angels fought, but they did not prevail, nor was a place found for them in heaven any longer. (Rev. 12:7-8)*

Gabriel

The name Gabriel means "man of God" or "God is strong." He is typical of messenger angels and is often used to reveal God's purpose and strategy concerning Jesus and His kingdom. He is generally portrayed in scripture as a man without wings and is referred to as "the man Gabriel..." (Dan 9:21).

Gabriel explained to Daniel the events of the seventy weeks of Israel (Dan. 9:21–27). He told Mary that the One born to her would be great and rule on the throne of David

(Lk 126-33). He explained to Daniel the future kingdoms of Medo-Persia, Greece, and Rome and foretold the untimely death of Alexander the Great (Dan 8:15–16). He announced the birth of John the Baptist to Zacharias (Lk 1:11–20).

In Daniel chapter 10, God responded to the prophet's prayer immediately by sending Gabriel with a message, but he was opposed by one of Satan's angels for 21 days. Gabriel required help from another angel (Michael) to get through to the prophet.

Cherubim

Cherubim are the highest order of angels, created with incredible power and beauty. They proclaim and protect God's glory and holiness.

Ezekiel described the appearance of the cherub Lucifer, before his rebellion:

You were the seal of perfection,
Full of wisdom and perfect in beauty.
You were in Eden, the garden of God;
Every precious stone was your covering:
The sardius, topaz, and diamond,
Beryl, onyx, and jasper,
Sapphire, turquoise, and emerald with gold.

The workmanship of your timbrels and pipes
Was prepared for you on the day you were created.
You were the anointed cherub who covers;
I established you;
You were on the holy mountain of God;
You walked back and forth
in the midst of fiery stones.
You were perfect in your ways
from the day you were created,
Till iniquity was found in you.
(Eze 28:12-15)

Cherubim are also known as the "Living Creatures" and are described by Ezekiel as having the appearance of four faces—a man, lion, ox, and eagle—four wings, feet like a calf, and they gleam like burnished bronze. Their appearance is likened to flashes of brilliant fire and lightning. They stand guard at the gate of the Garden of Eden, preventing uninvited guests from entering (Gen. 3:24).

Seraphim

Seraphim, which means "burning ones," are seen around the throne of God in the sixth chapter of Isaiah. Their ministry is closely connected to the throne and the praises of God. They are described as each having six wings.

Watchers

Watcher comes from an Aramaic word, `*iyr*, which means "vigilant, waking, watchful." This kind of angel is found in the fourth chapter of the book of Daniel in verses 13, 17 and 23. They put into operation plans that have been decided upon in heaven. They are vigilant and watch over the affairs of men.

When you're looking for angels, don't just look for beings that appear like men or beings with wings. They can appear in almost any form you can think of including ribbons and rays of light. Sometimes the only hint of the presence of angels is an unusual fragrance. Other times, it's a peculiar sound or a strong manifestation of God's glory. Be open to the many ways in which they can appear.

CHAPTER TWO

WHAT ARE THE COURTS OF HEAVEN?

WHEN I SPEAK ABOUT the Court of Accusation and the Court of Angels, I'm referring to locations in the realm of heaven. These places can be visited by us whenever we want. We travel there in our spirit. Our physical body remains here, while our spirit goes there and observes and interacts with beings that live in the heavens. Traveling in the spirit to heavenly courts may sound odd, but this is precisely the kind of experience that allowed the apostle John to write the book of Revelation.

The concepts of courts, justice and law, were not invented by man. They existed in heaven first, and over the millennia we learned of them and copied them. Our modern system of legal justice was modeled after the one found in the Courts of Heaven.

One of the Courts of Heaven is the Court of Accusation. (It's sometimes called the *Mobile Court*.) The Court of Accusation is where some of the legal proceedings of heaven are carried out. In this court, we're allowed to respond to accusations brought against us by evil spirits. A Judge hears the testimonies, we are cleared of guilt, and rulings (sometimes called mandates) are handed down.

We see glimpses of the courts and their proceedings both in the Old and New Testaments. The seventh chapter of the book of Daniel gives us a view of God as a Judge who sits upon a fiery throne, presiding over a heavenly court. In Psalm 82, the Lord says He judges among the hosts of heaven. In the scriptures, Jesus is portrayed not just as our Savior, but as our legal advocate or attorney:

And if anyone sins, we have an Advocate with the Father, Jesus Christ the righteous. (1 Jn 2:1)

Satan is portrayed as our accuser or the one who prosecutes us in the Court of Accusation:

Then he showed me Joshua the high priest standing before the angel of the Lord, and Satan standing at his right side to accuse him. (Zech 3:1 NIV)

What Are the Courts of Heaven?

Satan and his company of evil spirits have access to a court in heaven, and they know how to use it. They come there to accuse us. When we don't respond to their accusations, they torment us. This often manifests as sickness but it can affect our finances and other aspects of our personal life.

Satan accused Job in court. Job didn't appear there to be cleared of the charges, and as a result, Satan gained access to him. Job was afflicted with boils and his livestock and family were attacked. These are typical of the ways the enemy will attack when an accusation goes unanswered.

I know many people who have received prayer from faith-filled believers, and they haven't been healed. Some of them have experienced physical healing after appearing in the Court of Accusation. Others have reported sudden, positive outcomes in legal matters. There are many benefits to be gained by appearing in the Courts of Heaven.

In the same way that there are different courts on earth, each with their own jurisdiction, there are different courts in heaven, each designed to adjudicate different matters. Some of the places in heaven that are referred to as "courts" are more like councils. There is no judge present and there are no legal proceedings. The records of heaven are kept in the Court of Scribes, which is more like a library than a court. The Court of Angels is an informal place where you can be assigned angels to help you discover and fulfill the destiny God has prepared for you. As His child, you've been given access to these courts and councils. As you mature, you'll be introduced to other courts, you'll learn their purpose and you'll learn how to operate in them.

CHAPTER THREE

WHAT IS THE COURT OF ANGELS?

THE COURT OF ANGELS is a place where angels gather to meet with us. While there may not be a specific mention of the "Court of Angels" in modern Bible translations, there is mention of the "assembly" and "council" of angels in Psalm 89 (see verses 5 and 7).

When King Ahab planned to attack Ramoth Gilead, the prophet Micaiah was given revelation about a meeting in heaven where the Lord met with a council of angels (both good and evil) to decide Ahab's fate:

Then Micaiah said, "Therefore hear the word of the Lord: I saw the Lord sitting on His throne, and all the host of heaven standing by, on His right hand and on His left. And the Lord said, 'Who will persuade Ahab to go up, that he may fall at Ramoth Gilead?' So one spoke in this manner, and another spoke in that manner. Then a spirit came forward and stood before the Lord, and said, 'I will persuade him.' The Lord said to him, 'In what way?' So he said, 'I will go out and be a lying spirit in the mouth of all his prophets.' And the Lord said, 'You shall persuade him, and also prevail. Go out and do so.' Therefore look! The Lord has put a lying spirit in the mouth of all these prophets of yours, and the Lord has declared disaster against you." (2 Kng 22:19-23)

It's worth noting that a man, Micaiah, was allowed into the council meeting as an observer so that he might report what he witnessed to Ahab.

What I refer to in this book as the *Court of Angels* is more like an assembly or council than an actual courtroom. It's an informal place where angels meet with us and with the Lord for various purposes. It's always open. When you visit, you'll likely find that there are angels waiting there to help you.

CHAPTER FOUR

WHY SHOULD I APPEAR
IN THE COURT OF ANGELS?

THE COURT OF ANGELS is generally accessed after
we've appeared in the Court of Accusation. (Rarely, someone
will appear in the Court of Angels first, but they're usually
not aware that this is where they are.) Because the Court
of Accusation is the usual starting point, I'd like to first
explain why we may want to appear there and then discuss
why we may want to appear in the Court of Angels.

The Court of Accusation is suitable for hearing the most
common types of cases we're likely to be involved in. Any
believer may appear in this court. If you're sick, if you've
suffered a legal setback, if your business is hampered by
governmental red tape, or if in some other way God's plan

for your life is being opposed by an adversarial spirit, this is where your case will be heard. One reason why we appear in this court *first* is to learn how the Courts of Heaven function. Although the power of a verdict rendered in this court is just as powerful as any other court, the proceedings here are informal and special knowledge isn't required.

We may appear in the Court of Accusation for different reasons. Some appear there to have an illness removed. Some go there to have their finances restored. Some have the enemy's obstructions removed to legal proceedings, business dealings and contracts. This court can also be helpful when delivering an afflicted person from a demon.

Evil spirits normally respond to a believer operating in the authority of Jesus. When a demon does not respond the way we expect, there may be a legal problem that needs to be resolved. Appearing in the Court of Accusation may reveal the reason why a demon has refused to obey.

In our earthly legal system, when someone believes you've violated a law, they can file a report with the police and the appropriate court will hear the accusation against you. Your responsibility is to appear in court to answer the accusation. You may bring witnesses, and you may dispute the accusation, or you can admit guilt, but you must appear in court. If you don't appear in court, the judge will issue a warrant for your arrest. The warrant allows the police to come to your home or work and arrest you. Once they have you in custody, they will bring you before the judge to answer the accusation. If your case is heard and you refuse to appear—or if you do appear but refuse to respond to the accusation—you will be found guilty. Even if you are not guilty of the charges, a default verdict of guilt will be rendered if you fail to respond. The only way to be exonerated is to appear in court and respond to the accusation.

If you understand this process, it will help you understand how the Courts of Heaven function. The point to keep in mind is that if someone is accused and they fail to appear in court to answer the accusation, they cannot be exonerated, even if they are not guilty.

In most of the cases we'll encounter, an evil spirit will appear in the Court of Accusation and accuse us of some wrongdoing. When the accusation goes unanswered, the accuser wins by default. They then use this victory to continue to afflict or oppress us. Let's look at a case from the Bible that illustrates how this process works.

In the book of Zechariah, Satan appeared in one of the Courts of Heaven to bring an accusation against Joshua, the high priest. Joshua appeared in court to answer the accusation. The prophet Zechariah appeared with him to witnesses the proceeding. Here is how the case played out:

Then the angel showed me Joshua the high priest standing before the angel of the Lord. The Accuser, Satan, was there at the angel's right hand, making accusations against Joshua. And the Lord said to Satan, "I, the Lord, reject your accusations, Satan. Yes, the Lord, who has chosen Jerusalem, rebukes you. This man is like a burning stick that has been snatched from the fire."

Joshua's clothing was filthy as he stood there before the angel. So the angel said to the others standing there, "Take off his filthy clothes." And turning to Joshua, he said, "See, I have taken away your sins, and now I am giving you these fine new clothes."

Then I said, "They should also place a clean turban on his head." So they put a clean priestly turban on his head and dressed him in new. clothes while the angel of the Lord stood by. (Zech 3:1-5 NLT)

The Lord rebuked Satan and rejected his accusations. He then had Joshua's dirty clothing (sin) removed and had him dressed in fine clothing. Even though Joshua was guilty of the accusation, once he appeared in court and faced his accuser, the Lord was able to remove his guilt. The Court of Accusation is convened to hear accusations brought against us by evil spirits. It provides an opportunity for us to respond to and be exonerated of them.

When you appear in the Court of Accusation, you may receive an order from the Judge. Most often, He'll order a demon to stop harassing you. He may issue a written verdict to that effect. Typically, the order will appear as something like a scroll. Depending on the nature of the order, you may want divine help to carry it out. Angels can assist you in doing that. In some cases, the Judge may instruct you to go to the Court of Angels or the Court of Scribes. But even if He doesn't give you specific instructions, you may still want to visit the Court of Angels to see if you can obtain help.

I'd like to consider something the Lord revealed to Joshua during his appearance. He said:

> *If you will walk in My ways,*
> *And if you will keep My command,*
> *Then you shall also judge My house,*
> *And likewise have charge of My courts;*
> *I will give you places to walk*
> *Among these who stand here.*
> *(Zech 3:7)*

The Lord made a promise to Joshua. If he lived in a way that pleased God, he would be allowed to walk among the heavenly beings that he saw surrounding him. He would be allowed to visit with the company of angels and saints. This same opportunity has been given to us.

Motives

When we visit the Courts of Heaven, it's a good idea to be aware of our motives. Ask yourself why are you there? What are you hoping to accomplish? Who do you intend to meet? Why do you want to meet with them? Motives matter more than you might suspect. When your motives are pure, you will meet God:

> *Blessed are the pure in heart, For they shall see God. (Mt 5:8)*

Here are a few reasons (motives) why you may want to appear in the Court of Angels:

1. To bring an order (scroll) from the Court of Accusation for court-ordered enforcement.

2. To bring a scroll from the Court of Chancellors or the Court of Scribes for angelic fulfillment.

3. To ask for scrolls that have passed through heaven's governmental system on your behalf. These are orders that are waiting to be accepted by you. Angels can help you fulfill them.

4. There are governing bodies in heaven that are sometimes known as *benches.* If you become

a member of a bench, you'll be involved in governmental work. You may want to present your own mandate from a bench to the Court of Angels for angelic assistance.

CHAPTER FIVE

HOW DO I APPEAR IN THE COURT OF ANGELS?

ALTHOUGH IT MAY SEEM like we would need great prophetic insight or well-developed spiritual gifts, visiting the Court of Angels is easier than you might imagine. In the same way that you have a physical body which exists in the physical world, you have a spiritual one that exists in the spiritual world. Your spiritual body can engage the spiritual world at any time. The spiritual world includes the realm of heaven and its courts and councils. Most of us have been taught that we can't go to heaven until we die. The truth is, if you've been *born again* by the Spirit of God, you have access to heaven right now. God the Father dwells there. Jesus said that He is the door to the Father. We can access heaven any time we want, through Him.

Our spirit has a set of senses that closely approximate the physical ones. Activities in the spiritual world are perceived through these senses. Angels are often perceived as images we see in our mind. Their communication is received as thought impressions or words and phrases that we hear in our mind.

Sometimes our spirit will sense the presence of an angel and our mind will interpret it as a faint, glowing shape, a colorful ray of light, sparkles, or other visual impressions that emit light. Sometimes we'll smell a unique fragrance they carry or hear an unusual sound indicating their presence. It's easy to dismiss these cues as figments of our imagination. But these subtle appearances of light, sound, fragrance, and touch are often the manifestation of angels.

Angels can carry the glory (or presence) of God. The manifestations of God's glory are diverse. Some people feel an ecstatic joy; others feel a weighty sensation. I tend to sway back and forth when I'm in God's glory. Being in the presence of angels can cause increased manifestations of glory.

Where to Begin

The first indication that you may want to appear in the Courts of Heaven is when prayer seems to be of little use.

How Do I Appear in the Court of Angels?

Whenever you sense that God's will is being obstructed, consider going to the Court of Accusation and asking if there is an accusation being brought against you by an evil spirit. Appearing there is a simple process.

The first step is to address the Judge and ask for the court to be convened. You can think this in your mind or you can say it out loud. The next step is to ask for your accuser to appear.

When your accuser appears, you may sense its presence in any number of ways. Some people see an image in their mind of a creature. I often see something like a dark cloud beside me. You may hear a voice speaking in your mind. The accuser will appear in a way that will let you know it has arrived in court. Be prepared to face more than one accusing spirit. The number of accusers you may see and how they appear will be different for each person. In addition to multiple accusers, there may be a company of angels present in court.

The Court of Accusation achieves justice differently than courts on earth. In an earthly court, being exonerated is done by disputing accusations. In the Court of Accusation, we do not dispute accusations. Every one of us has sinned. We are all guilty. But Jesus died for our sins. The blood that was shed when He was crucified removes our guilt. We're exonerated by letting His blood take away our guilt.

I'd like to clarify one point. You do not need to go to the Court of Heaven to be justified in God's eyes. The day you believe in Jesus as your Savior, you are made righteous in the sight of God and nothing more needs to be done. The courts do not affect your relationship with God. They deal with the relationship you have with your adversary. Vindication before your adversary comes when you allow the blood of Jesus to be your response to an accusation. Jesus is your attorney. His blood is your defense.

In general, there is one strategy you'll want to employ when responding to an accusation. Jesus gave us part of that strategy in the Sermon on the Mount:

"Agree with your adversary quickly, while you are on the way with him, lest your adversary deliver you to the judge, the judge hand you over to the officer, and you be thrown into prison." (Matt 5:25)

Notice in this passage that Jesus referred specifically to officers of the courts. When responding to an adversary in the Court of Heaven, never dispute an accusation. To do so may lead to serious consequences and as believers, it's not necessary. Simply agree with the accusation and move on to the next part of the process.

After you've agreed with the accusation, acknowledge that the blood of Jesus is your defense. You can do this in a number of ways, but you're simply stating the fact that you come before the court not in your own righteousness, but in the righteousness provided by the blood of Jesus. You're allowing His blood to impute its righteousness to you. This removes your guilt, takes away the effect it had on you, and silences your accuser.

If the accusation involves repetitive patterns of ungodly behavior that are likely to bring further accusations and force you to return to court, it's a good idea to repent of the behavior.

After you've heard the accusation and responded, it's time to receive your verdict. Sometimes the Judge will render a verdict immediately. I've heard many people testify that as soon as they confessed their sin and repented, the Judge banged His gavel and declared them "not guilty." In some cases, you may need to ask for a specific verdict or decree. The nature of your case and to some degree, your familiarity with the courts, will determine your actions. There is nothing wrong with simply accepting a not guilty verdict from the Judge. This will be sufficient to release you from demonic oppression or affliction. However, it's been my experience that asking for a specific verdict can be helpful.

If for example, you're being harassed by a particular spirit, such as a familiar spirit, you may want to ask the Judge for a Decree of Divorce. Such a decree makes it illegal for that spirit to come near or harass you. If your case involves a legal proceeding here on earth, you may ask the Judge for a decree that specifies the outcome of that case. If your case involves contractual issues, you can ask for a scroll that outlines the terms of the contract. The Judge may, at his own discretion, give you a scroll even if you do not ask for one.

Along with asking the Judge for a specific decree, you may want to ask for supporting documents that are pertinent to your case. My purpose in asking for documents is twofold: First, the documents remind me that I've already obtained the victory. I can also use them to remind my adversary that he's been defeated and he had better leave me alone. Both the Old Testament prophets and New Testament Apostles were given documents (scrolls) to eat. There is more than just a symbolic gesture in this. A scroll from heaven is a divine spiritual order or ruling. The intent is that it becomes part of our spirit. To that effect, after I receive a scroll or document I often make a physical gesture of taking the scroll in my hand and placing it inside my spirit. (Similar to what Ezekiel and the Apostle John did when they were given scrolls to eat.) Some of my friends have been directed to eat a scroll after they received it.

Once you've appeared in the Court of Accusation, the Judge or Jesus may direct you to visit the Court of Angels to receive help. The Court of Angels is located near the

Court of Accusation. You should be able to locate it by looking around in the immediate area.

Do you perceive a large door in front of you? If so, try to open it. Do you see flashes of light or luminous figures? Do you perceive a weighty presence? Do you feel currents of air moving around you? Do you perceive voices speaking to you in your mind about the things of heaven? Any of these can indicate that you're in the presence of angels.

Going Directly to the Court of Angels

Another option is going to the Court of Angels without going to the Court of Accusation, first. This is done by engaging the heavenly realm through your mind, or what some would call, your imagination. You can close your eyes, or leave them open if you're able to perceive the spiritual world that way. To the best of your ability, set your heart and mind on visiting the Court of Angels. Wait for a few minutes and observe what happens in your mind or note what you see in the spirit.

CHAPTER SIX

MANDATES AND THE COURT OF ANGELS

WHEN YOU APPEAR IN the Court of Accusation, you may ask the Judge for a ruling. Rulings are sometimes referred to as orders, scrolls, decrees or mandates. They're rulings from heaven about your life. They have information about your divine destiny or calling.

A mandate often appears in the form of a scroll. If you receive one, you can take it to the Court of Angels and ask for help enforcing it. The Court of Angels isn't difficult to find. It's usually very close to the Court of Accusation. Just look for a gathering of angels when you leave the court or look for a very large door that sometimes has light showing through or around its edges.

Once you've located the Court of Angels, you might hold the scroll up and ask if any angels would like to volunteer to help you fulfill its mandate. Typically, a group of angels will step forward. Sometimes one of them will assume a place of leadership. Once the company of angels is formed, they usually leave the courtroom with you and you may not see them again. You can assume they're doing what is necessary to help you follow through.

Mandates can come from other courts like the Court of Chancellors. Whenever you receive one, if you need angelic help, you can go to the Court of Angels.

You may find mandates in the Court of Angels that have been delivered there from higher courts. These orders are waiting for you to accept and assign to angels for enforcement. The nature of these assignments can be almost anything including revival, healing, and finances. If you can think of a job title, there are likely to be angels that are equipped to carry out that type of assignment.

If you're not certain about how to proceed in the Court of Angels, you might simply ask Jesus for guidance. You can go to the Court of Angels as often as you'd like.

CHAPTER SEVEN

INTERACTING
WITH ANGELS

IT'S NATURAL TO BE amazed when you first sense the presence of angels. Be aware that these spiritual beings are our servants. We co-labor with them to help establish God's governmental rule over the universe. Acknowledge their presence and do your best to treat them as supernatural co-workers. Respect them, but avoid becoming too enamored with them. An obsession with angels can take your focus off Jesus. There's nothing wrong with communicating with angels. Just be sure to keep the relationship in the right perspective.

Angels are spiritual beings. Spiritual communication doesn't use the physical structures of the human body.

Angels do not have eardrums, lungs, and a nervous system like we do. Communication with them is done through the transmission of thought impressions and visual imagery. Your spirit receives visual images and thoughts which are sensed in your imagination and interpreted by your brain as words and objects that you may recognize.

Learning to communicate with angels takes a bit of practice, but much of it is intuitive. Some people have developed their ability to sense the thoughts of angels. They carry on conversations just as they would with any human. Communicating with angels might seem strange at first, but with practice, it will become more natural.

When I pray for someone to be healed, I often assign an angel to go to the one I'm praying for. Sometimes I assign the angel a specific task like removing a demon or a device that inflicts pain which was placed there by a demon. I don't generally hear the angel respond when I give it an assignment. It isn't necessary for me to hear them. I usually observe (in my mind) a glowing body of light moving away from me. I assume it's an indication that the angel heard me and that it's doing what I asked it to. I don't *know* that's what's happening with certainty. I *trust* that it's happening. As with everything we do that is supernatural, an amount of faith is required. Sometimes we must simply believe that angels hear us and that they're obeying our instructions.

CHAPTER EIGHT

TESTIMONIES FROM THE COURT OF ANGELS

I HAVE MANY FRIENDS who have visited the Court of Angels. Some of them were kind enough to share their testimonies. These testimonies are not intended to create rigid rules about operating in the Court of Angels. They're provided to help you understand just a few of the things that are possible. Our first testimony was shared by Sheila Young during a social media discussion that I hosted about the Court of Angels. The interesting thing about this testimony is that as Sheila was reading other people's testimonies, she went to the Court of Angels:

I've never been to the Court of Accusation. While reading this post, I went there! I was found not guilty right away. The scroll was handed to me by someone. I went to the Scribe's Court and got my copy. Then I went into the Angel's Court. I've never been there that I'm aware of. They yelled, "Sheila!" They took my scroll. I was so thankful for the angels and their obedience to God.

As I was with the angels, I had an overwhelming feeling of many more accusers. So I went back to the Court of Accusation. There were many accusers there that yelled, "liar!"

I pled guilty. God instantly said, "You're innocent."

So I repeated the process. This time, the angels knew I was coming back. They were there, waiting for me. I handed off the copy of the scroll and they took it. I think they got on my case right away.

Thanks to all who helped me get there today. God bless each of you!

The next testimony was shared by my friend Gary Wood on the same discussion that was mentioned above.

I have only dealt with the Court of Angels once. I had some scrolls/mandates that I needed action on. The Court of Angels was my third stop. I went in and saw a lot of angels kind of milling around. I asked for five reaping angels. I really had no idea if there was such a thing but five assembled in front of me. I handed them all a copy of my mandates and explained what I needed individually from them. They took the scrolls and seemed to nod with understanding about what I wanted but they didn't really say anything. I wasn't sure what if anything else needed to be said so I kind of awkwardly thanked them and left.

A man shared with me two testimonies of his son's trips to the Courts of Heaven that occurred after he read my book *Traveling in the Spirit Made Simple.* This is the account of his second appearance, where he learned that he is allowed to receive help from angels and that Jesus is willing to testify on our behalf.

Our son went to the Court of Heaven last night on behalf of an acquaintance who is struggling with a ministry and two jobs. Struggling with the busyness of it all—and the lack of finances. Here is our son's testimony. The man he represented will be called "Steve."

I appeared at the Mobile Court and walked down a series of steps and up the center aisle to the defense table. There was a gallery of people present to witness the proceedings. I noticed everyone, even the Judge, had smiles on their faces like they were eager to proceed. I said, "I bring the case of Steve in (a city in the US) before the court. Where is his accuser?"

A small cloud of darkness appeared for a few seconds behind the prosecutor's table and then a demon materialized. I asked the Judge, "What are the charges against Steve?"

Hesitant to respond, the demon muttered the word "selfish." He repeated it over and over and over again. After hearing "selfish" at least twenty times, I looked at the Judge and asked Him with a thought, "Can we make this guy stop?"

He mentally replied, "He's delivering the accusation, let him finish."

Finally, after about thirty repetitions of the word, the demon then added "self-serving," and was finished.

I said, "Open the book!" The bailiff pulled out a large, square, red leather-covered book. He opened it, and it was full of writing. I realized I needed a witness, so I said, "I call Jesus Christ to the witness stand." Jesus appeared and sat down at the witness stand. Even in the midst of the proceedings, I was struck by the love that radiated from His gaze. I asked him, "Steve is holy, righteous, and blameless before you, is that not so?"

Jesus replied, "It is so."

I asked, "Steve is justified before you, is that not so?"

He replied, "It is so." The demon, who had initially glared at me when I called him to appear, was now glaring at the ground. Jesus came down from the witness stand and seated Himself in the gallery.

I asked the Judge for a verdict. He pulled out a scroll and began writing on it. When He was finished, He sealed it and beckoned me to approach the bench. He handed me the scroll and as I took it, I asked, "Do I need to read this scroll?"

He replied, "No, you don't need to read it, but you do need to know that Steve's opposition has been condemned."

I thanked Him, then turned and walked out of the courtroom. I went to the Court of Scribes next and walked in. I approached a desk and asked the scribe there if he could copy the verdict I had just received. He said he would, and I handed him the scroll.

I walked around as I waited, marveling at the amount of wisdom recorded there. I realized that not only were court's verdicts recorded there, but there were also multitudes of records of conversations that were held by saints that the Lord had heard and was pleased by. I stood there in awe, realizing the attentiveness of the Lord to His people. The scribe reappeared with the verdict scroll and handed it to me. I thanked him and walked out of the Court of Scribes.

I then entered the Court of Angels. Angels were everywhere, conversing and awaiting assignments. I came to a halt in the middle of the room and all the angels were looking at me. I held up the scroll and asked, "Who will go enforce this verdict?"

A large angel stepped up. He was the biggest angel in the room. He was about twelve feet tall and had a massive sword at his waist. He said, "I will go." He turned and motioned to four other, smaller angels who gathered behind him. They left the court to carry out the verdict and then I left the court.

Our last testimony comes from my friend, Sue Beckman.

There are several courts in heaven. All of heaven is waiting for the sons to come into maturity so that we can begin to take responsibility in these courts. I know that many people are beginning to utilize the Mobile Court, (Court of the Accuser) but this is just the beginning. There are a few of us here in the Northwest that are operating in the courts and making legislation. Anna Wingate is one whose mandate is to train and equip people to form "benches." Benches are a vitally important part of working in the courts.

*After having about five people die from different forms of cancer, I asked the Lord–no, I **pleaded** with the Lord—to show me the key to getting rid of this awful disease. I was on my face in tears. I knew there was something that I was missing. Five months later, I was introduced to Mike Parsons and the Courts of Heaven. I was given a large key ring and a box from the Lord. Each time I get a revelation, that "key" goes on the key ring and in my box that I have on my throne in heaven.*

I'm currently mentoring people who want to grow deeper in their relationship with God and who desire to grow into maturity as His sons and daughters.

So I've helped folks go into the Court of the Accuser (Mobile Court) to get some issues taken care of. I've also been called by God to intercede for a good friend with their permission, and go to the Mobile Court.

My friend, who I'll call "MT," was diagnosed with Leukemia about three years ago. He went through chemotherapy and a bone marrow transplant. He was doing well and coming along. Then, a month after I was at Mike Parson's conference here, MT had a setback. His wife asked people to pray. So, with fear and trembling, I went to the Mobile Court.

Jesus met me outside the courtroom. He asked if I was ready. I thought to myself, "about as ready as I'll ever be." He laughed. So, the doors opened, and I walked into the courtroom and saw a table on the right. That was where Jesus and I sat. I could see the Judge's bench, and God was seated there. I had the sense that he was pleased. Jesus asked me why I was there. I told Him that my friend MT had a set back with his treatment. I wanted to get to the core of what was going on, so I was there to represent him. I was ready to hear the accusations from the enemy and if needed, to go back in his generational line to take care of any issues that may be blocking his healing.

Jesus smiled. He was pleased that I stepped up. So, at that point the accuser was called in. I was not afraid. Not at all. In fact, I felt so at peace. Jesus is our advocate, so I had nothing to be afraid of. I stood and told the court that I was standing in for MT, representing him. I was there to hear the accusations. I told the court that I wanted a divorce from cancer and any of its bedfellows.

The accusers were called in. I stood and listened to all these accusations from each of them. There were three demons throwing out accusations. I took notes. Once they were finished, I turned to the bench and said, "I plead guilty on all counts. I ask the court for mercy, and I renounce and repent for what has been said. I stand under the Blood of Jesus that was shed for me. I now ask for the court's judgment."

I waited. God opened the book. I could see things written in it. Then, He waved his hand and the writing disappeared. He then closed the book. He looked at me, and the gavel went up and slammed down and He said, "Not Guilty! Fully healed." The divorce was granted.

I remember smiling and turning to Jesus. I thanked him for all he had done. He hugged me and said,

"Well, done! I think I will be seeing you more here, won't I?"

I replied, "You better believe it!"

Then, God called me to the bench. I walked up. He asked me if there was anything else I needed from the court. I thought for a moment, then said, "Yes, sir. I request no host versus graft complications and that MT will not suffer from this—that he would no longer suffer from Leukemia or any other cancer. "Healed!" He shouted. And with that, I was handed a scroll.

I took that scroll and went to the Court of the Scribes to have it recorded. Then, I was given the original scroll back along with a copy that was to be taken to the Court of Angels.

I went to the Court of Angels. As I walked in, the whole place was full of angels. When they saw me, they stopped and turned and waited. I said I needed two healing angels to go to MT to stay with him and work on his healing. There was to be no graft versus host disease, and he was to be healed of his leukemia. There were many angels who raised their hands saying, "Pick me!" I chose two and gave them their scroll. They immediately left. I then took my scroll and put it in my heart. I knew if I needed to go back into court, I would have it at hand.

A year later, I received an email from MT's wife, stating that he was back in the hospital and his health was failing. His blood counts were off and his organs were beginning to fail. They even called in family members that were overseas to come home. I saw that email and I was incensed! I immediately went back into the court. Jesus was there. He had a grave look on His face, but He was glad to see me. I told him why I was there and he smiled. "Good job." I hadn't done anything yet, but I was ready to. I said, "If there's something that I missed or didn't repent of, please let me know." He smiled and said, "It's all okay."

I approached the bench with boldness. I told the Lord that I have a Divorce Decree from leukemia and any other complications that may come and from graft versus host disease. I told the judge that the accuser is in contempt of court because MT's health is failing. I stated that I had a verdict of "healed."

I pulled the scroll out of my heart and presented it to the court. As God took the scroll from me, he had a look of pure pleasure on his face. I had no idea why until a few minutes later. He read the scroll and called the accuser in. The demon was shackled and could not speak. He was escorted in by two huge angels. They stood him before the bench. "I find you in contempt of court. You have broken the Divorce Decree that was given." Then, He turned to Jesus and said, "Son, take this demon to the void."

I had no idea what that meant. What I did see, however, was the demon squirm in the arms of the two angels holding him. Jesus came over and led the two angels that were holding the demon toward a door on the left. Then they were gone.

I stood there and wondered what just happened. God turned to me and said, "My dear, Sue. This is how this court works. If you find after you have been given a verdict, that the enemy has tried once again to come and do something, you immediately come back to court. They are found in contempt of court, and I will deal harshly with them, especially in this type of case. You have done well and I am proud of you."

Within half an hour after going back to the court, I received another email. "Praise God! MT's counts are getting back to normal. His kidneys are functioning again."

I read that and wept with JOY! This heavenly court stuff really works!

I've received many more testimonies from friends who have appeared in the Court of Angels. Some people are willing to teach others how to do it. But you don't need to know much about procedures and protocols before you go there. Most of what you need to know you'll learn when you get there. It's a safe place to learn and you're encouraged to ask questions. Go there in faith. Expect to meet Jesus and the angels. Get to know your heavenly home a little better.

CHAPTER NINE

CLOSING
THOUGHTS

GOING TO THE COURT of Angels can be an effective
strategy to gain victory over the enemy. It's also a way to
begin learning about heaven's governmental system and our
place in it. As God's children, we are heirs of His kingdom.
Our inheritance isn't something we receive when we die.
We've already received it—Christ died and rose from the
grave. In doing so, He resurrected our dead lives with His
and seated us with Him in heavenly places. Since we've
been seated with Him in the heavens, shouldn't we be about
our Father's heavenly business?

Growing in spiritual maturity demands that we learn how
to operate not just in the Court of Angels but in even

higher courts, such as the Court of Scribes, the Court of Chancellors, and the Divine Council. God wants us to grow into mature sons. (In heaven's vernacular, we're all sons, and we're all brides.) Becoming a mature son requires us to administrate His kingdom from our seats of authority in the heavens. Operating in the Court of Angels is intended to lead us on to these important responsibilities.

It is my prayer that as you explore the Court of Angels, you would learn to cooperate with them, that you would develop a greater understanding of the courts and councils of heaven, that you would enter into a more intimate relationship with Jesus, and that you would fulfill your divine destiny as a mature son of God.

THANK YOU FOR PURCHASING THIS BOOK

For inspiring articles and an up-to-date list of my books, go to my website, **PrayingMedic.com**. There you will also find links to my Podcasts and other resources.

Defeating Your Adversary in the Court of Heaven

Are believers really able and allowed to appear in the court of heaven?

Many Christians are surprised when they first hear that the courts of heaven are real. Many more have been shocked at how their lives were changed after they appeared in court to face their adversary. Illnesses have vanished, legal proceedings have been halted and demonic attacks have suddenly stopped.

Isn't it time you learned how to present your case in the court of heaven?

With the same down-to-earth teaching style used in Divine Healing Made Simple, Praying Medic explains in layman's terms what the courts of heaven are and why we may want to appear in them. He shows why, when and how you can appear in the court of heaven and how you can obtain victory over your accuser. There's even a simple, step-by-step protocol that shows you exactly what to say, when to say it, and what not to say.

Emotional Healing in 3 Easy Steps

If you've been through counseling, prayer, or deliverance, but you're still plagued with painful emotions like shame, guilt, fear or anger, this book can help you get free of those emotions once and for all.

This isn't another nice-sounding, but powerless self-help book. It's not filled with pop-psychology. It's a field-tested method of erasing traumatic wounds in your soul and releasing the painful emotions associated with them. And it doesn't require long hours of prayer or counseling. You can do it yourself and it will only take a few minutes.

If you're ready to ditch your emotional baggage, put your past behind you, and get off the emotional roller-coaster you've been riding, you're just 30 minutes away from a new you.

Are you ready?

Divine Healing Made Simple

Get honest answers to the difficult questions you have about healing and the supernatural:

- Why are my prayers ineffective when I ask God to heal someone?
- Many people have prayed for my healing— so why am I still not healed?
- Does God want me to learn a lesson through physical suffering and sickness?
- I was miraculously healed through prayer— why have my symptoms returned?

Get the answers to these questions... and many more.

In his down-to-earth style, Praying Medic presents a solid case that all believers have power and authority from God for healing. Miracles are happening every day through the prayers of average men and women on the street and in workplaces. With a little instruction, you too can learn how to release God's healing power. Exercises at the end of key chapters will help you develop your ability. With insight on many other topics including making disciples, deliverance, words of knowledge, and how God speaks to you through your dreams, this book celebrates what God is doing and shows you how miracles can become part of your everyday life.

This book is part of a series called **The Kingdom of God Made Simple** —
a self-study course designed to train believers to live the
life offered to them as heirs of God's kingdom.

Seeing in the Spirit Made Simple

Is "seeing in the spirit" only for a few people—or can anyone do it?

If you want to see angels, demons and the heavenly realms, but have been told you don't have the gift of seeing in the spirit, this book is for you. For years we've been told that seeing in the spirit is a gift given to only a few special people or an anointing that must be imparted to us by a man or woman of God. In this book, Praying Medic presents biblical and physiological evidence to prove that seeing in the spirit is not reserved for only a few special people, but is possible for everyone.

With the same down-to-earth teaching style he used in **Divine Healing Made Simple** and **Hearing God's Voice Made Simple**, the author provides Bible-based teaching, dozens of testimonies, and illustrations that reveal the truth about seeing in the spirit. He includes exercises at the end of key chapters to help you improve your spiritual vision. Whether you're a seasoned seer or a newbie, you'll learn from the experiences and insights shared by the author. Not only will you develop better spiritual eyesight, but your relationship with God will grow too.

This book is part of a series called **The Kingdom of God Made Simple** — a self-study course designed to train believers to live the life offered to them as heirs of God's kingdom.

Hearing God's Voice Made Simple

Is God Really Speaking?
Yes—and you can learn to hear Him.

Today, many are skeptical that God is speaking or that we can know with certainty we're hearing Him accurately. **Hearing God's Voice Made Simple** makes the case that God is speaking and that we can learn to hear Him. As you read this book, you may even discover that God has been speaking to you all along but you simply didn't know how to hear Him.

With the same straightforward, down-to-earth style used in the best-sellers **Divine Healing Made Simple** and **Seeing in the Spirit Made Simple**, Praying Medic teaches about the many ways in which God speaks. You'll find practical exercises at the end of key chapters to help develop your ability to sense what God is saying to you. Whether you're skilled at hearing God's voice, or more of a novice, this book will show you ways of hearing from God that you may not have considered—and you'll also learn what to do with the things God says.

This book is part of a series called **The Kingdom of God Made Simple** —
a self-study course designed to train believers to live the
life offered to them as heirs of God's kingdom.

Traveling in the Spirit Made Simple

Is spiritual travel "astral projection" or is it a biblical practice used for God's purposes?

If you've been taught that traveling in the spirit is unbiblical or is only used by the New Age or the occult, this book is for you. The author examines accounts from the Bible which demonstrate that the prophets and apostles traveled in the spirit. He compares astral projection with Christian spiritual travel and proves that they are not the same thing. Far from being an occult practice, spiritual travel is actually a tool given to us by God to accomplish His divine purposes.

With the same down-to-earth teaching style used in **Seeing in the Spirit Made Simple** and **Divine Healing Made Simple**, Praying Medic provides Bible-based teaching, dozens of testimonies and illustrations that will help even the least experienced believer understand spiritual travel. Exercises are provided at the end of key chapters. Traveling in the spirit can help you in healing, deliverance and intercession, but most importantly, it will help you know God in a more personal way.

This book is part of a series called **The Kingdom of God Made Simple** — a self-study course designed to train believers to live the life offered to them as heirs of God's kingdom.

My Craziest Adventures with God - Volume 1
The Spiritual Journal of a Former Atheist Paramedic

Does God speak today? Would He heal the sick or work miracles through you—even if you feel "average" or not particularly gifted?

Not long ago, Praying Medic was an average guy who sat in a church pew every Sunday wondering if there was more to the Christian life than this. After losing his job, being divorced and being kicked out of his church, it seemed like his entire world was going up in flames. Then one night in a dream, God asked him to pray for his patients. When he awoke in the morning he knew nothing would ever be the same.

Come along on these intriguing adventures as an ordinary paramedic confronts his own skepticism and fear and learns how to hear the voice of God. Get to know Praying Medic, the author, through these stories from his personal spiritual diary. Watch as he learns how to pray for his patients and for strangers in the marketplace.

God's goodness and sense of humor are revealed in these true stories. And you'll witness the transformational power of God as it changes a hardened skeptic into a man of real faith. These stories won't just encourage you—they'll teach you how to live daily in the fullness of God's kingdom.

My Craziest Adventures with God - Volume 2
The Spiritual Journal of a Former Atheist Paramedic

Picking up where **Volume One** left off, Praying Medic and his wife are back with more stories about their supernatural adventures with God.

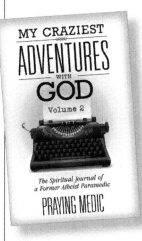

Not long ago they were a couple of atheists. Then they met God. After learning about the authority and power believers have been given to heal the sick and work miracles, they began praying with people wherever they went and their lives have never been the same.

Come along on their adventures with Jesus and the Holy Spirit. Discover how an unexpected invitation to travel to Brisbane, Australia, brought them into working on the streets—alongside dedicated local church volunteers—praying for men and women in homeless shelters and on the streets.

Watch as these ordinary believers see the sick healed, the mentally ill set free, and demonic forces beaten. From healing, to automotive miracles, time alteration, and financial miracles, nothing is off limits for God.

You'll be laughing one minute and crying the next as the extravagant love of God is poured into the lives of the people you'll meet in these stories.

A Kingdom View of Economic Collapse

If you'd like to learn about economic collapse, but you're tired of being lured into investing scams, and hearing warnings about God's judgment, this may be the book you've been looking for.

In his usual no-nonsense style, Praying Medic gives readers a crash course in economics and finance, explaining things in terms the average person can understand. He provides an overview of historic cases of economic collapse and determines which nations are at risk today. He examines the cause of the recent Greek debt crisis and shares the lessons to be learned from it. He shares a number of prophetic dreams about economics and finance, and offers suggestions about how we might rebuild after a collapse, if one were to happen. The final chapter discusses how the kingdom of God ought to respond to crisis.

Topics covered in this book:
- God's purposes for economic crisis.
- Why governments print so much money.
- A prophetic look at our economic future.
- A simple lesson on finance and economics.
- The role of the International Monetary Fund.
- A look at historic cases of economic collapse.
- How central banks and the Federal Reserve operate.
- Which nations are currently at risk for economic collapse.
- How we might rebuild in the aftermath of an economic collapse.
- How the Greek debt crisis happened and lessons to be learned from it.

American Sniper: Lessons in Spiritual Warfare

Drawing upon scenes from the popular film American Sniper, Praying Medic gives readers a look inside the mind of a well-prepared kingdom soldier.

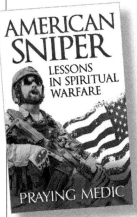

Relying on the use of analogy and symbolism, the author compares the life of a Navy SEAL to the life of a believer. The book closely follows the script of the film. With each scene the author illustrates principles of spiritual warfare, drawing from his own life experiences and from many spiritual dreams he's had.

The goal of this book is to help believers assess their state spiritual preparedness and identify any deficiencies they might have. Resources are recommended for further training and equipping, if needed.

Because so many lives have been devastated by the kind of emotional trauma portrayed in the film, the last chapter includes a simple approach to healing emotional trauma that can be used by virtually anyone.

Whether you're in a position of church leadership or just someone who wishes to be better trained and equipped for ministry, this book will add a few more tools to your arsenal.

21865502R00043

Printed in Poland
by Amazon Fulfillment
Poland Sp. z o.o., Wrocław